From Darkness to Light

An inspiring story of one man's 25 year struggle and victory over drug and alcohol addiction

By

Randy Riggs

ISBN: 1-4107-6798-1 (e-book)
ISBN: 1-4107-6797-3 (Paperback)

This book is printed on acid free paper.

1stBooks – rev. 07/31/03

Acknowledgments

This book has been a long time in the making, and I am indebted to a number of people who have encouraged me and who have contributed to this project in some way. I have had several people read this manuscript in different stages who have made suggestions that strengthened the material significantly. Several people whom I have a great deal of respect for, read this story and told me that it was one that needed to be heard.

I wanted some different people from different faiths to read this and make sure that the content of the story wasn't too harsh for the average person. I in no way wanted this book to glorify the life of a drug addict or alcoholic. My intention for writing this story was to do just the opposite and convince our youth that this life is to be avoided at any cost. For those that are still suffering, I wanted to show them that there is hope and there is a way out.

I want to give special thanks to my brother Ricky, who being well educated helped me to edit and do everything necessary to make this story readable. I would also like to give thanks to a loving mother who never gave up on me. I want my three children Jamie, Ryan, and Nicole (Coco) to know how grateful I am to them and how much I love them. They are the greatest blessing I have in my life.

I would encourage anyone to read this story, but would like to suggest that if you start it, please finish it. The best part is in the end.

I would also like to acknowledge the many leaders and missionaries of the Church of Jesus Christ who helped and encouraged me along and made it possible for me to be where I am today.

1.

After being in bondage to drugs and alcohol for several years, I was approached by the missionaries from the Church of Jesus Christ of Latter Day Saints. At that time, I was facilitating meetings in their substance abuse program and was asked if I could write a brief summary of some of the experiences I have had in my life. Over the years I have experienced so much good and so much evil it's incredible. Before I start, I do want to say that in spite of it all, I'm here and my life is good. My being here to share this story with you is a miracle in itself. To keep this brief will be difficult and I pray to God that he will help me write the things that will be of most benefit to those who read this.

I want to start by introducing myself. My name is Randy Riggs and I'm an alcoholic, a drug addict and a compulsive gambler. Just about anything that you can do that's addicting, I've probably done it. Recently, I celebrated my seven-year anniversary of being completely clean and sober; an accomplishment I seriously believed I would never obtain. Before I share some of the rich experiences the Gospel of Jesus Christ has brought to my life and how I have been able to walk away from what, at times, seems nothing short of a terrible nightmare, I would like to share with you how I started down a long, dark path that led to endless trouble, torment, discouragement, despair, and total destruction.

I started this journey when I was quite young, about 12 or 13 years old. Up to that point my life was good. I had a good family, two older brothers, a younger brother and a younger sister. That put me right in the middle. Our family was close; we did many things together. We had family prayer, we all went to Church together, and we even had family home evening a few times. We went on several family vacations and did all the things that every kid should be able to experience.

My dad was a faithful priesthood holder and I lived what I thought was a pretty normal childhood. I pretty much followed the pattern that good LDS boys follow. I was baptized and confirmed a member of the Church of Jesus Christ of Latter Day Saints at the age of eight, ordained a deacon at the age of twelve, and a teacher at the age of fourteen. It was sometime shortly after being ordained a deacon that things started to change in my normal world.

My parents started having problems with their marriage. I'm not going to blame all the hardships I have had in my life on my parents for not being able to work out their marriage differences. I often wonder, however, how different things might have been if they would have stayed together. My mom was a stay-at-home mom who was always there for us no matter what our needs were. She seemed to always be there when comfort or nurturing was needed. She was very active with her church callings and somehow managed to put up with all the aggravation that five children can create. My dad got up every morning and went to work. He worked hard and it seemed that we always had plenty for our needs. When they couldn't make it work any more, divorce was the final outcome.

My mom, who didn't have a career and had never worked since she got married, was all of a sudden thrown into the working world. Not having enough money was a constant struggle for her. She took a minimum wage paying job in Salt Lake City, and even with that and the child support my dad paid, it just never seemed to be enough. Quite often my mom had to rely on the church for food to feed the crew she now had to support. Times were tough, but mom always tried to keep us from seeing the difficult situations she was dealing with. She worked during the day and was usually home an hour or two after we got home from school. The stress my mom was under everyday was sometimes more than she could bear. I could always tell when she had been crying.

3

Not having a dad around when you're in your teens was tough. He did come and pick us up on weekends but it wasn't the same as being the happy family we once were. There was an emptiness I felt daily in my life. I began doing a lot of different things to try and fill that empty void in my soul. I started hanging out with the wrong crowd at school, started smoking cigarettes. I just wanted to belong or feel like I was part of something. I was accepted quickly and pretty soon I had more new friends than I knew what to do with. They weren't exactly the kind of friends my parents would have wanted me hanging out with, but for some reason I really didn't care what they wanted anymore.

My two older brothers were going through pretty much the same thing. One day my oldest brother Dale asked me if I wanted to smoke a joint (marijuana cigarette). I was totally shocked that my brother was smoking weed. I figured if he was doing it, it couldn't be that bad. This was my first encounter with drugs. It really didn't do anything for me and I remember how nasty it tasted and how bad it made me cough. I told a couple of my friends at school about it and they told me that the first time that you smoke weed you needed to smoke a lot just to get off. Being the curious type of person I am, I couldn't wait to find out what it was like to get high. One of my friends at school said he had a big brother who could get us a bag of weed, so we all put our lunch money together and had him get us some. Back then they didn't weigh it out like they do now; they just threw some in a bag and called them

4

lids. For ten dollars we bought about a half an ounce or so.

My brother Dean and I got together with my friend on a Saturday and went to a hideaway spot we had, took a pipe, and set out to find out what it was like to get high. We smoked about six or seven pipe loads and I still wasn't feeling any different. After about two more I started feeling more different than I had ever felt in my life. We all started laughing at stupid things and didn't stop for at least two or three hours. We were so messed up we were afraid to go home. My brother and I finally decided that we had better go, so we left and went home. We were so wasted that you could spot us from a mile away. My mom could tell that something was up and started asking what was wrong with us. We really couldn't hide what was going on and admitted to her that we had smoked some pot. She called my dad, and of course he came right out and we did the old "take a cruise in the car with dad" routine. They made a big deal out of something that we felt was no big thing.

So began an extended trip down a long, dark and gloomy path that ended up lasting 25 years of my life. 25 years is a good chunk of anyone's life. If we were all to live 100 years, that would be one fourth of someone's whole mortal life. Most of us won't live to see 100 years, so 25 years is a long ride.

2.

After that first encounter with pot I couldn't wait to get high again. For my two older brothers and all my friends in school, smoking weed was becoming a daily thing. We'd always meet early in the morning and get high before we went to school.

Pretty soon, being the entrepreneurial kids that we were, we could see that there was money to be made, so we started buying pot in quantity and selling lids. We had a pretty profitable little business going.

It wasn't long before my first encounter with the police. I was in ninth grade and I was outside having a cigarette one day when one of the teachers came outside and saw me smoking. He asked me to give him my cigarettes. I told him I didn't have any. He stuck his hand in my coat pocket and pulled out a container I had that was full of weed. He dragged me to the principles office and he called the cops. That was the first in a long list of arrests that I would have in my life. It still didn't stop me from doing what was rapidly becoming a way of life. One thing I can honestly say about pot is that it gives you an attitude where you just simply don't care. You don't care about school, you don't care about work, and you don't care about anything except getting high.

My grades went from honor roll status to barely passing. Along with getting high every day and going to school, my attendance at church dropped to zero. When the weekends would come, we'd load up and head for the mountains. Camping out was a great way to get away from it all and allowed us a way to escape, to get high, or whatever we decided was good for the weekend. Around this time I was introduced to another one of my worst addictions, drinking. This one I carried right to the end. I loved drinking beer probably more than any other addiction I had. I remember saying several times that I could give up all of my bad habits, but I would never give up beer. Here I was 15, 16 years old, and the most important thing in my life was making sure that I always had a way to get high or drunk.

Before long I was introduced to acid (LSD), mescaline, and mushrooms. Psychedelics were always what we thought were a lot of fun and I indulged heavily. Acid was always a recreational drug for us and was usually saved for times when we weren't around any type of civilization; mainly because when you dropped acid you were so completely obliterated for eight to twelve hours, you didn't want to be anywhere where you would have to maintain the appearance of being normal. However, there were a few acid trips we took where we did it and went to school, or had to go home and face our parents. That was always an interesting experience. At that point in my life I figured that life was just one big party. It didn't matter if you were at school, out of school for the summer or whatever. There was always some way, or somewhere, you could go to get totally wasted.

During this period of my life I managed to get arrested about three or four more times, for alcohol related offenses: public intoxication, illegal possession of alcohol and a couple of other misdemeanor charges. By the time I hit high school I had tried about every kind of drug there was except cocaine and heroin. Those I would save for my later years. I don't believe I could even put a number to all the parties I went to: keg parties, rock concerts, parties in the mountains or in someone's backyard, barbecue get-togethers. It didn't matter what it was, if there were alcohol and drugs involved, I'd be there.

3.

I don't remember exactly when it was in all of this confusion that I came to know that I was developing a serious problem, but at the time I simply didn't care. My junior high and high school years were one big party. I had developed a reputation of being one of the school bad boys and I always thought that I was cool and that I was doing the cool thing. The church friends I had when I was younger had drifted away. They were still there; they just didn't want much to do with me. My two older brothers and I had developed quite a reputation in our neighborhood and I know that a lot of our old friends' parents had told them to stay away from us.

One day my oldest brother Dale decided to alter his draft card to make him twenty-one so we could buy beer. The store clerk could tell it had been altered and called the cops. Because it was a government ID card, they made a federal case out of it and took him away.

My brother had had a couple of run-ins with the law already, so they gave him a couple of choices-prison or military. He didn't like the idea of being locked up so he joined the U.S. Coast Guard. We gathered up all of our friends and had a huge going away party for Dale, and off he went. That left my brother Dean and me to carry on the Riggs tradition. We continued doing what we did best: party, party, party.

My brother Dean had made it all the way to his senior year in high school and half way through it, he figured he had had enough and decided to drop out. I never did quite figure that one out. It was at this time that he started buying pounds of weed and my friend Kim and I were selling it in mass quantities at the high school. We even had a couple of kids selling for us at the junior high schools. We were also selling acid, mescaline, PCP and any other drug we could get our hands on.

The emptiness I always felt inside was still there, it never went away. No matter how much alcohol I poured in, or how many drugs I did, I was never able to fill that empty void. I was going against everything I believed in and was walking down a path that was against everything I had been taught. I remember so often the guilt I felt after having a long weekend of partying. I know now that these feelings of guilt I always felt inside were whisperings of the spirit, trying to make me aware that what I was doing was wrong. I simply did not care and chose not to listen.

4.

My brother Dean and I shared a room, and one night when we were almost asleep, we heard the doorbell ring. We heard my dad's voice. He made his way downstairs to our room. I couldn't figure out why he would be there at this time of the night. He came into our room and turned the light on and told us that our brother Dale had been involved in a boating accident in the Gulf of Mexico and had drowned. He was dead. I couldn't believe this was real. I went upstairs and my mom was crying and my Uncle Ralph was there trying to calm her down. This was my senior year in high school. We were all devastated. How could all of this be happening? My brother was only twenty. He was way too young to die. Dale, Dean and I were always so close; we did a lot of things together. When Dale would come home on leave he'd say hi to everyone and then it was off to the mountains for a 3 or 4-day party. Now he was gone. The emptiness was even bigger now.

Dean also had his share of run-ins with the law. One day he was in Salt Lake trying to steal beer off of a beer truck and was caught and arrested. We had an uncle who was a Sheriff in the Salt Lake Sheriff's office. He decided that it would be best to leave him in there overnight and give him a taste of what jail was all about. If you've never been in county jail before, it is definitely no picnic. This was probably the best thing that could have happened to Dean because it gave him a chance to take a good, hard look at his life and see where he was headed. He didn't like what he saw and decided that it was time to make some changes. He walked away from all of his friends and started going to church again. He ended up going back and doing what he had to do, to get his high school diploma. A few months later he told me that he had turned in his paper work and was going on a mission. Dean shocked a lot of people when he did this, but no one was more surprised than I was.

Meanwhile, nothing had really changed in my life. I was still partying like a madman, drinking, smoking weed, dropping acid, snorting PCP, and smoking angel dust. You name it and I was doing it. My life was a mixed-up mess and I really didn't care. I was rapidly becoming an addict to the drugs I was doing and to the alcohol I was drinking.

Alcoholism and drug addictions are serious, progressive diseases. The only way they get better is if you can give them up entirely. Unfortunately, most people that have these diseases won't give them up until something compels them to. I was no different. I was in the beginning stages of my addictions and had no idea what kind of heartache and disappointment I was headed for. I reflect back to those times and remember so many instances where I can honestly say that I knew in my heart there was a better way, I just simply chose not to listen. The still, small voice that you hear in your heart will always lead you to do good, but you do have to listen to it. It tells us in the scriptures that the Lord is no respecter of persons; he loves us all equally and wants nothing but the best for all of us. I can testify to the fact that Satan is no respecter of persons either and will gladly take us by the hand, one by one, and lead us down that long, dark path of destruction. There is a scripture in the book of Mormon that reads "and thus we see that the devil will not support his children at the last day, but doth speedily drag them down to hell." (Alma 30:60)

5.

It was right around this time that I met the woman that would become my first wife and the mother of my three children. I was a senior in high school and was doing what was necessary just to get through. I know now that if I would have put forth a little effort and tried to do good in school, I could have excelled academically, and who knows, I might have been able to get a scholarship to college. Once again, I just didn't care.

After I graduated from high school I got a job in a department store in Salt Lake City and worked in the garden shop for about $3.00 an hour. It wasn't long after this that my girlfriend came to me with news that she was pregnant. Here I was, freshly out of high school, working for nothing and my girlfriend was pregnant. I wasn't even ready to grow up and be an adult yet and I was faced with a situation that would change my life forever.

It was very difficult to break the news to her parents. Her father was second counselor in the bishopric in our ward and she was only fifteen years old. He asked me if I had given any thought to temple marriage. I hadn't even thought about marriage, let alone temple marriage. I was 18 and she was 15 and she was 5 months pregnant. The date was set and we were married that January. You would think that bringing a child into this world would have shaken me to my senses and settled me down, but I was so caught up in my addictions I couldn't stop.

I continued to party with all my friends and didn't slow down at all. I lost my job at the department store and got a job through my step-dad with an ice company in Salt Lake City. I worked hard at any of the jobs I had and was able to pay the bills, but it seemed like we always struggled financially. My wife also enjoyed partying, so between the two of us we continued doing things we both knew were wrong. She never seemed to have the problems with drinking and doing drugs like I did but she still enjoyed partying.

We had our first baby that summer and named her Jamie. She was a beautiful little girl and she brought a lot of joy into our lives. At the same time, my drinking and partying was getting more and more out of control. PCP was very popular at this time so I was doing a lot of that, selling it, and also selling pot. My partying was starting to create problems in my marriage. I was constantly going out on drug deals, leaving my wife home to take care of the baby while I was out partying, going to rock concerts and carrying on. I was the only one out of all my friends that was married, so a lot of the time the parties would end up at our house. We were finally able to move out of the basement apartment we lived in and bought a mobile home.

One day my friend Kim and I were drinking and had done about eight valiums each and my wife wanted to go to a big party in Salt Lake. I was in no condition to be behind the wheel of a car that night and to this day I don't remember any of this. At the end of the night we were getting ready to go. I was passed out at the party from all the drinking and drugs I had done. My friend Kim picked me up, carried me outside, shook me around a little and put me in my car. The next thing I knew we were in the emergency room at the hospital. My friend Kim was lying next to me on a table with his face full of glass. He had smashed his face into the windshield upon impact. They had to call in a specialist to remove the glass from around his eyes because they didn't want him to lose his sight. I was running around with a bump on my head and stitches in my lip trying to find out what had happened and where my wife was. I had run my car head-on into a parked semi.

My wife was in intensive care and bleeding internally. Kim was in serious condition. My wife was very petite at the time and had turned side ways when she saw that we were going to run into the truck. She was very seriously injured and here I was, barely hurt. My father-in-law and my step-dad went in to

19

where my wife was laying and they gave her a priesthood blessing. Her internal bleeding stopped and she was taken out of intensive care that day. I heard it from more than one doctor that it was a miracle that she had survived. **It was a miracle**; a miracle given to a faithful priesthood holder who simply did not want to see his daughter die. I know for a fact that it was his faith and the miraculous healing power of the priesthood that saved her life that day.

I couldn't believe that all of these things were happening. When I walked out of the emergency room that morning, a police officer came up and told me that the paramedics had taken blood from me at the scene of the accident. They knew that I had been drinking heavily and arrested me for driving under the influence. This would be the first of 4 DUI's I would receive.

After this incident, I swore up and down that this was it and I was going to change my ways. I was done drinking and I was done doing drugs. I swore to my wife, my parents, her parents, and everyone else, that I would change my life.

I stayed clean for a little while, just as I did several times throughout all of this, but I was never able to stay that way for long. I had a court date and had to hire an attorney. Being that this was my first offense after becoming an adult, the judge was pretty lenient on me. I was given a fine, had my driving privileges restricted, and had to go to drug and alcohol counseling.

At this time I was introduced to my first AA meeting. Going in there and listening to all the stories was an incredible experience. These people had totally ruined their lives. Some of them had lost everything; their jobs, their families, and their self-respect. I sat there thinking that these people were way serious wastes of life. They had lost it all. I was totally amazed that anyone could allow him or herself to get this out of control with their drinking. I walked away from that meeting shaking my head thinking, "I certainly am glad that my life isn't that messed up." It wasn't yet, but I was certainly headed that way.

I did make a valiant effort to change my ways and stayed clean and sober for probably two or three weeks. After everything blew over and things went back to normal, I figured it was ok to start drinking again, only this time I'd keep it under control.

My restricted driver's license allowed me to drive at work or otherwise I would have been out of a job. It was about 6 months after all of this happened, on an Easter Sunday, that my wife and I and a bunch of our friends decided to go to a club in Bountiful for a few drinks. My restricted driver's license didn't allow me to drive on Sundays so my wife drove.

We ended up staying pretty late that night and by the time we left, everyone was pretty messed up. Nobody was sober enough to drive, but that never seemed to stop me. We made it about a mile or so and we got pulled over. This was my second charge for

21

driving under the influence. Once again they took me away and locked me up. This time it was a little more serious. I was driving on a restricted license and it was my second offense.

I hired the same attorney and had to go to court again. This time they came down pretty hard on me. They took my license away. I had to go to Davis County Mental Health for alcohol counseling, was fined severely, and had to go to jail for a weekend. The punishment I received in court was only the tip of the iceberg. I had to pay astronomical lawyer fees, and my insurance rates went sky high for having two DUI's on my record.

6.

My brother came home from his mission about this time, and had heard about all the trouble I was getting myself into. Whenever he was given the opportunity he always tried to interject a little religion into our conversations. I had to make a run to Cedar City and St. George one day at work and asked him if he wanted to go along for the ride. Dean and I were always very close, so it was good to see him and spend some time with him. Of course he preached to me all the way there and back, but that was ok too. We talked a lot about the good old days and all the crazy things we did when we were younger. The funny thing was, I was still doing a lot of it. He did everything he could to convince me that there was a better way. I felt the spirit strong that trip and knew that what he was telling me was true; I guess I just wasn't ready.

The spirit bore witness to me several more times on that trip, that if I didn't make some changes soon, worse things were in store. The spirit will never lead you astray and will always point you in the right direction if you'll only listen. One thing I have learned over the years is that we are all given our own agency to make our own choices in life. Our father in heaven will never take that away from us. There is one catch; we all have to pay the price for the choices we make. My brother and I are still very close. I guess he just figured it out a lot earlier in life than I did. His life and the way he progressed forward proved that.

I was growing tired of my job driving truck; it was always the same old routine. I never set goals in my life. I had no plans to further my education, therefore my whole life seemed like a hopeless dead-end. I had no direction. As long as I had a 12-pack of beer in the refrigerator or money to buy some if I didn't, that seemed to be all that mattered to me. I look back now and it's amazing how everything I did in life was centered around my drinking and drug addictions.

My wife and I spent a lot of time camping in the summers. When we went shopping, the first thing in the shopping cart was beer and cigarettes. If it meant we had to buy less food, that was ok. My wife's family had a lot of get-togethers on holidays and on other occasions. We would get in big fights all the time because I hated going to them. They were all good, active Mormons and I didn't fit in. All of her sisters and their husbands would come and they'd sit around and talk about their church callings. All I wanted to do was get out of there so I could drink my beer and smoke my cigarettes. A lot of times I'd start a fight on purpose just to get out of going.

My wife was rapidly getting tired of me, and having to deal with all of the problems that my addictions were causing. I had quit my job because I was tired of it and decided I could make a career change and start selling life insurance. What a mistake that was. I was making no money at all and she was working and basically supporting us at this time. She came home on several occasions and I'd have friends over partying, or she'd come home and I'd be passed out on the couch. Our marriage was headed for trouble and I knew I had to do something or I was going to lose her. My brother had met a lady, got married, and moved to Las Vegas. We stayed in touch and he was trying to talk me into moving there and going to work with him. He had joined the union in Vegas and was setting up trade shows and conventions. I had gotten him involved in selling insurance, so he was also doing that.

I had discussed the possibility of moving to Vegas a few times with my wife and decided that it was coming to the point where it was my only option if I was going to save my marriage. I figured that if I got away from all of my friends I could change my life and stop partying and drinking so much. We had a big keg party in our back yard and said goodbye to all of our friends and took off.

We found a nice two-bedroom townhouse to rent, moved in and within one week had met all kinds of new friends. The insurance business wasn't doing well, so my wife and I both signed up with the teamsters union in Vegas and worked there when work was available. The trade show industry in Vegas is big, but it's all union and if you're high on their list you can work pretty steady. If you're not, then you don't work very steady at all. Between my wife and I, we were barely making enough to pay the bills. We had met a lot of new friends and in no time at all we were hitting the clubs, bars, and casinos. It didn't take long at all and I was right back where I left off when I was in Utah.

My wife and I were fighting worse now than we ever had. I finally couldn't take it any more, so I called her dad in Utah and told him to come and get her. He came down that Saturday, loaded her and Jamie up and took off. I continued working trade shows and conventions, but work was scarce and I struggled just to make ends meet. I had way too much free time on my hands and started drinking worse than I ever had.

With my wife and daughter gone, I never felt as empty inside as I did then. Not only was I drinking lots of beer, I started hitting the hard stuff and was drinking almost a fifth of whiskey every night. I had a difficult time sleeping and didn't eat much, so whiskey and beer became my way of escape. My brother was working a lot steadier than I was. He had been doing this kind of work a lot longer than I had. He knew the right people so he managed to make a pretty good living doing what he was doing.

7.

My brother was married in the temple, went to church every Sunday and paid his tithing. I know now that that was the biggest reason he was able to do so well. He was doing everything he was supposed to in order to receive the blessings that come from above to those who live their lives accordingly. In the meantime, I wasn't doing well at all. I was drinking myself to death, had no money, my rent was coming due and I didn't know what I was going to do. I missed my wife and Jamie, so I called my mom and asked her if she could come down and rescue me. She and my step-dad came down that next week and loaded me up and off we went.

The geographical change didn't work. When you're an addict you're an addict and no matter where you run to, your addictions go with you. I could have moved to the other side of the world, where I didn't know anyone, and within a matter of days I would know whoever I needed to know to support all of my bad habits and addictions.

I moved my stuff into my mom's basement and lived with her for a while. She and my step-dad worked for the Union Pacific Railroad and thought they might be able to get me a job working on a traveling steel gang. I got the job and hired on in Layton, Utah. It was the hardest work I had ever done, but I was very grateful to be working again. I started seeing my wife again and we started to spend a lot of time together. I wanted more than anything in the world to be back together again as a family.

We went out together one night for dinner because she said she had something important to discuss with me. I was hoping more than anything that she wanted to talk about putting our lives back together. After we discussed the possibilities of that happening she told me that she was pregnant. I was surprised, but happy at the same time. I was making good money working for the railroad so we found a nice place and moved in. For the first month or so I was able to come home every night because we were still working close enough to home. As we got further and further away, I eventually had to move on board the bunk cars. The bunk cars weren't bad to live in, but they definitely weren't what you would call home. I couldn't stand being away from home so much, but I did what I had to do.

I got a good friend of mine a job working at the railroad, so at least I had someone to hang out with.

On weekends we'd come home and I'd get to see my wife and Jamie and then on Sunday we'd head back. My friend Shawn and I spent a lot of time drinking while we were gone and I think we hit every bar in Southern Wyoming. One weekend when we were home visiting our families I came up with an idea. I had a friend in Salt Lake that had access to about any kind of drug you could think of. I figured I could invest a little of the hard-earned money I was making and make some money on the side. I picked up a pound of weed and a couple of ounces of mushrooms. When I got back to the bunk cars, I sold out in less than one hour. I could have sold more if I would have had it, so this became another way of making a little side cash. All I had to do was make sure I picked up right before payday.

It seems like throughout the twenty-five years I was using, I always found ways to get into selling whatever drugs were popular at that particular time. Not only was it a way to make extra money, it always provided a way for me to get my drugs free.

I worked on that gang all the way up through Wyoming until we reached Cheyenne. I had put in papers to see if I could get transferred to a section gang in Salt Lake City, or anything else that became available that was closer to home. An opening did come up for a gang in the Salt Lake yard, fixing track and replacing railroad ties, so I took the offer and moved back home. That job was a great one because it paid well and I was close to home. The problem was, it didn't last long and I got laid off. That September my son Ryan was born. I was very happy to have a son and both my wife and I were happy to have him as the newest edition to our family.

Here I was again, laid off. This time it wasn't for long. My friend Kim and his dad had a painting and sandblasting company and happened to need some help, so I went to work for them. Being a painter wasn't the greatest job in the world, but it paid the bills and that was all that mattered at the time.

8.

When I had worked for the ice company in Salt Lake, I always thought about starting my own ice business. I spoke with my step-dad about starting our own business and we did it. We called the company Rocky Mountain Ice. We started out with very little money and one truck and I went to work. I went up and down every street in Salt Lake City passing out business cards and letting everyone know that we were in business. It took a while and a lot of hard work, but between my step-dad and I, we built a pretty good business.

It wasn't too long after we started the ice business that my wife and I had our third child. We named her Megan Nicole. We nicknamed her Coco. Coco was a beautiful little girl and once again, she brought a lot of joy into our lives. I cherish the relationship I now have with all three of my children. It wasn't always that way. There was a time when my addictions to drugs and alcohol had made it so even my kids had no respect for me.

It was shortly after Coco was born that we bought a house in Woods Cross. The ice business had grown a lot and at times it was all I could do to keep up with it. The first two years we were in business I wasn't able to take any time off. In the summer months I was putting in 12 to 16 hours a day, 7 days a week.

Being in the ice business, I was delivering to a lot of parties and special events. It gave me plenty of opportunities to do what I did best, drink. There were several times I would wake up in the morning and not remember coming home the night before. I was drinking so much that I was starting to black out. I used to keep a 12-pack of beer or more in my truck at all times. Why not, I had the biggest ice chest in town. I delivered to parties, special events, restaurants, private clubs and bars. As you can imagine I was always wasted.

It was about this time that I was introduced to what I consider the worst addiction I ever had, cocaine. Every time we went to parties, cocaine was always available. I was always afraid of doing coke and tried to stay away from it; it was also very expensive. I think by now I knew myself pretty well, and knew that if I did it, I would like it too much and then I'd have another addiction to take care of. I was right. We were at a party one night and I ended up buying some. I didn't think it was worth it because it really didn't do a lot for me. It was probably because I had been drinking too much that night and coke and alcohol kind of counteract each other. We ended up buying some more another night. Once I got off on coke I figured I had found the best drug in the world. I loved the way it made me feel. You could do coke, stay up all night, drink more than you were ever able to before, and be the life of the party. As far as I was concerned cocaine was it. So I thought. Cocaine rapidly became the worst nightmare that I have ever lived through.

I started out buying little amounts, a quarter gram here and a quarter gram there. Nothing I thought was too serious. Pretty soon quarters weren't enough and I was buying half grams, grams, and more. It was right about now that I started having some real serious problems with my marriage. I was coming home late all the time, partying like crazy, and my wife had finally had enough. I came home late one night and she threw me out. I stayed at my mom's house that night but returned the next day. I told my wife that I was making the house payment and if she wanted out of our marriage she could leave. We stayed in the house together for another two weeks or so and then she left. I came home from work one day to find out that she and my kids were completely moved out. She had rented a truck while I was gone, got some friends to help her and she and the kids took off.

I sat down on the floor in my empty living room and couldn't believe this was happening to me. I did what I always did in situations like this: I called up my best friend Kim and started drinking. We ended up killing a couple cases of beer that night. Once again, I sat there in that empty house; my wife was gone, my kids were gone, and I never felt as lonely and empty as I did now.

I had a couple of friends move in to offset the rent, and within a couple of weeks I had furniture again, friends to party with, and life went on.

Pretty soon I couldn't keep up with the cocaine habit I had developed so I did what I always did to support my habit: I started to sell it. I started buying eight balls (eighth of an ounce), then quarter ounces, half ounces, ounces. I was making twice as much selling coke as I was selling ice 12 hours a day.

My habit was getting so bad that after a while I was snorting up all of my profits. Soon it got to the point that I was running two receipt books at work. I did this so I could extort money from the business to support my habit. It seemed like no matter how much cocaine I shoveled into my system it was never enough to fill that empty void I had inside.

One night, a friend of mine stopped by to purchase some coke. He asked me if I had ever free-based coke. I had heard of it, but never tried it. This was back before you could buy crack cocaine on the streets, or at least I hadn't heard of it yet. When you free-base coke, you heat it up with a little baking soda until it cooks down to pure oil. As soon as it cools down, it turns into a rock. You then get a glass pipe and put as many screens in it as you can and smoke it. This friend of mine who introduced me to doing coke this way, introduced me to the worst nightmare I ever lived through. The rush you get from doing it this way is unbelievable. The problem is that it only lasts a short time and then you spend the rest of the night chasing that same rush. You can never quite get it again. You crave it so bad it's unreal. There's not a drug out there that makes you crave it like this does, not to mention how bad it messes you up.

There is a lot of danger in doing coke this way because it's very easy to do too much and a lot of people end up dying. I know that I came close several times. Problem was, I didn't really care if I died or not. After you've been doing coke this way for a while you start to get real weird. You start seeing shadow people, you start to hear and see things all the time. You develop a paranoia that is worse than any nightmare imaginable. You'll spend all night running through your house, sweating like crazy, looking out windows, running up and down stairs, looking in closets, hearing things, and locking yourself in the bathroom. This has to be as close as you can get to being completely and totally insane. It is never enough to make you stop though. You still spend all night chasing and trying to get that same rush. I had friends that would do this and spend the whole night running around their house with loaded guns looking out windows. It's amazing they didn't kill someone.

As if this wasn't bad enough, one night my curiosity got the best of me and I started shooting coke in my arm. This is something that a lot of my friends were doing, but I swore up and down that I'd never stick a needle in my arm, and now, here I was, doing that too. As far as I'm concerned this was about as bad as it gets. Now I was shooting coke, running around my house looking out windows all night, in constant fear that the FBI, DEA, or the police were outside. I know that if someone normal could have seen this, I probably would have been declared legally insane.

I kept selling coke to feed my habit. I found new sources to buy from so I would have other places to go when one source would run out. I was embezzling thousands of dollars from my own business to support my habit. My life was crazier now than it had ever been. Crazy was a good word for it. I should have been locked up in a mental institution. Even when my kids were at my house, I'd still do it. I'd lock myself in my bedroom while they were watching TV, or I'd wait for them to go to sleep, and stay up all night doing it. I didn't know it at the time but Satan had me right where he wanted me.

9.

One night I picked up some of the strongest cocaine I had ever had. I was by myself and prepared a very large amount to do. I knew when I drew it up that it was way more than I should do, but I didn't care. I did it anyway. I didn't even get the needle out of my arm when I collapsed and went down. The room was shaking so bad I couldn't believe it. I was in violent convulsions on my living room floor and couldn't stop. I heard voices in my head, evil voices. I know now, just as I knew then, that this was the voice of the devil. I was closer to dying than I had ever been. I was alone so there was no one to help or to call for help. I spent the next 10 or 15 minutes fighting with everything I had to stay alive. I finally stopped shaking long enough to crawl to my bathroom. I lifted myself up with the help of the toilet. Once I was up I held on to the bathroom counter and shook for at least another 5 minutes or so. The whole time I could still hear the voices in my mind. I finally came out of it.

Believe it or not, as soon as I knew that I was ok I loaded up and did another one. This was definitely the closest I had ever been to death. It is by the grace of God that I'm still here to even tell this story.

The girl I was going out with at this time worked at a private club in Bountiful. We had a system down and she moved a lot of coke at the club for me. She was a cocktail waitress, so when somebody wanted to buy some, she would bring it to them with their drinks. They would pay her like they were paying for their drinks. It was a successful system and I turned a lot of coke at that club. I don't believe that she really liked me near as much as she just had an addiction like I did, and was willing to do what ever it took to take care of it.

There were always plenty of women around when you had coke. It kind of went with the territory. I always had my pick of women back then, as long as I had the drugs they were looking for. Even though I wasn't legally divorced yet, I thought that being single was the greatest thing in the world. I had more money than I had ever had, I had all of the drugs and alcohol I could handle, and had my pick of about any woman I wanted. Life was good, or at least I thought it was.

I was sitting home one night taking it easy when the phone rang. It was my girlfriend and she was working late that night. She wanted to stop by after work and buy a half a gram of coke from me. I told her no problem, and I decided to stay up for her. The club closed at 1 a.m. so I figured she'd be by sometime around 1:15 or so. She didn't show up until about 2:30. When she arrived I let her in and we talked for a bit. She acted very nervous but I didn't think much about it.

She asked if I had the half for her and she handed me sixty dollars. I thought this was kind of strange because she never paid me for any of hers. I usually gave it to her because she sold so much for me at the club. Besides, a half was only fifty dollars. She told me to keep the change. She asked me if she could use the bathroom. She went into the bathroom and all of a sudden I heard a big crash. I got up, walked down the hall, and the cops were coming in all over the place. My front door was lying on the floor. Before I knew it I was face down on the floor with a gun to my head. They pulled her out of the bathroom and handcuffed her too. They had to make me believe that she was also getting arrested. I had just been set up and I knew it. They made me lay down on my couch, face down, handcuffed, while they tore my house apart looking for drugs. I'd been pretty busy that night and sold pretty much all that I had, so they didn't find a lot of drugs. They did take a couple thousand dollars in cash off of me, including the three twenty dollar bills that she gave me that were marked. They also found glass pipes, torches, syringes, and all kinds of other paraphernalia. One of the cops knew me pretty well and just shook his head. He asked me what Dorain (my step-dad) was going to say when he found out.

Once again, I sat in Davis County Jail after they booked me, wondering how my life had gotten so messed up. A lot of people would have decided after they'd been through the things I'd been through, that it was time to do something different, to seek help, or find some way to change what was happening in their life. I really was tired of my life. I felt so hopeless, such a waste. I guess I just didn't know what to do to change it all. I was in total bondage to the addictions I had. I sat in jail until morning and called my mom to bail me out. She couldn't believe what was going on. My mom is the greatest mother in the world. She told me all the time how she didn't approve of the things that I was doing, but would always love me, no matter what. It tore her apart to see the stupid things I was doing. I was in some real serious trouble this time. I called my attorney and let him know what had happened. He got a copy of the police report and it was all there. My girlfriend had been arrested a couple of weeks before and made a deal with the cops to set me up. They tried to get me to make the same deal and set up some of the people I was dealing with, but I wouldn't do it.

I went back to work and a couple of guys from Denver came into our office one day and said they were interested in buying our business. The business was all in my step-dad's name, so I didn't have much say in what went on. My step-dad was getting past retirement age and he was tired of working so much. Selling out sounded like a good idea to him. They made the offer and he accepted it. They assured him that I would remain working there as manager, but I knew that as soon as summer was over with, they'd probably lay me off.

10.

A short time after all of this happened, I was with my friend Kim and we went over to the bar one night to have a few drinks. I still hadn't gone to court yet for the drug charges I was facing. I was sitting at the bar that night. I guess I was thinking that if I drank enough, all of this would go away. I kept drinking and drinking. By the time I left that night I was so drunk I couldn't even walk. We got in my car to go and only made it about a mile. The red lights came on. I was so drunk I almost fell on my face getting out of the car. When the cop came up to me, I couldn't even talk. They handcuffed me and took me away. That was DUI # 3.

I called my mom again from the jail and told her I didn't care if she came and bailed me out or not this time. I just wanted her to know what had happened. I was in so much trouble I didn't know what I was going to do. I stayed in jail the rest of that night and all the next day. Around 7 p.m. the jailer told me I was being released. I came out and my dad was there to bail me out. After I was released we talked in his car on the way back to my house. I was in a lot of trouble and didn't feel a lot of hope in anything. I think at this time I just wanted my life to end. I'd had enough. I couldn't see any way that I was going to get out of this one without doing some serious time in jail. I was going through an ugly divorce, I was facing felony drug charges, my house payment was behind three months, the bank was ready to start foreclosure proceedings, and to top it all off I just got arrested for my third DUI. I don't believe I ever felt as empty and hopeless as I did at that moment. The worst thing about it was that no matter how hard I tried, or how bad I wanted to, I couldn't give up doing the things that were creating all the problems in my life. The drugs, the drinking, selling coke; my life was so messed up and I didn't know what to do to make it all stop.

I called my attorney again and he couldn't believe what I was telling him. I went home that day and my house was as big a mess as I was. I just laid there trying to figure out what I was going to do. I went to work the next day and one of the guys that worked for me told me that he would catch up the payments on my house and assume the loan if I wanted to do that. I figured it was a good way to get out of one of my problems. I spoke with my ex-wife and told her that if she didn't sign the papers I was going to move out and the bank would foreclose. It was her choice. I didn't really have a lot of options. My life was a total mess and I couldn't deal with all that was going on. I guess that's one of the reasons I kept drinking and doing drugs more than ever. It was the only way, I figured, I was going to keep my sanity.

I was over at another one of my favorite bars on the other side of Bountiful having a few beers exactly two weeks after I had been arrested for my third DUI. Once again, I was drinking like I was crazy. I think I figured if I drank enough that maybe I'd get lucky and die. I just kept drinking. I didn't care anymore. The bar closed at 1 a.m. I got in my car to leave. I didn't have a driver's license because they had taken it the last time I got arrested. I didn't even make it a block and the red lights came on and this time it was the North Salt Lake Police. DUI #4.

They called the paramedics to take blood from me because the Breathalyzer wasn't working. I refused to let them take it, which was an automatic admission of guilt. At this point I really didn't care. I didn't care about anything. I just wanted this to end. I don't remember how I got out that night. All I remember was going home and going to bed. I woke up and was hoping that all of this was a bad dream, but it wasn't. This was my life. I figured that this was pretty much it. I was in so deep now that there was no hope. I decided to get up, get myself dressed, and go to work. All I had left was my job. As soon as I got to work, my boss Charlie called me into his office. I didn't know why he was calling me in. He had a very serious look on his face and started asking me if the rumors he was hearing were true. He had heard about all of my

Randy Riggs

arrests and DUI charges. I told him that they were true. He tried to act as sorry about all of this as I was, but I knew it was all an act. He told me that they had some pretty strict rules about drug related offenses and he was going to have to let me go. I turned in my credit cards, keys, and my truck and walked home.

My house was just down the street. I walked into my house, headed for my bedroom, and pulled my 30-30 rifle out of the closet. I pulled out a few bullets and loaded it. I must have sat there for two or three hours looking down that long barrel. I started flashing back through my life remembering everything. I remembered a lot of the good things that had happened in my life that seemed so long ago and I remembered all of the bad. I kept hearing voices in my head telling me to just go ahead and get it over with, end it, what's the point in going on? There is no hope; your whole life is a waste. I grabbed that rifle and started thinking about my kids. What would they think? What would they feel? They would have to spend the rest of their lives knowing that their dad blew his brains out in his bedroom. I threw the gun down and started crying. I just didn't know what I was going to do, but taking my own life was definitely not the answer.

11.

I decided that I had better call my attorney. Once again, he couldn't believe what I was telling him. He told me that if there was anything at all I could do at this point, it was to go check myself into an inpatient drug and alcohol treatment center. He gave me a name to call at the Davis County Mental Health Clinic. The man's name was Harold. I knew Harold from when I had gone to drug and alcohol counseling before. I gave him a call and explained what had happened. He asked me if I could make it up to his office to see him.

I went to his office and spent an hour talking to him. He told me that he had suffered just like me at one time and was a very serious alcoholic. He asked me if I was ready to make some changes in my life, and if I was, was I ready to do whatever was necessary to make those changes come about. I told him that if I didn't do something quick, I was either going to end up dead, or spend the rest of my life in prison. He made a phone call to an inpatient treatment center in Clearfield. They had one bed available. He told me to go home, get some personal things, pack a bag and get over there. I went home, packed and called my mom to see if she would give me a ride.

When I walked into that treatment center I really didn't know what to expect. They were just getting ready to have lunch so they showed me to my room, where I'd be staying for the next month or so, and asked me to join them. I was introduced to everyone and after lunch they showed me around. They had a list of chores for everyone to do and told me that I would be responsible for cooking breakfast for everyone.

This place was like a big house. It had a big living room area, where they had group therapy three times a day, a good-sized kitchen, an office for the counselors, bathrooms and two big rooms where everyone slept. I figured that this would be a breeze and that I could skate through all of this with no problem. I was definitely in for a surprise. When they told me I'd be responsible for cooking everyone's breakfast, I had no idea that it would be at 5 a.m. I was used to drinking myself to sleep every night, so I didn't sleep too well that first night. That wasn't near as bad as trying to get up and running at 5 a.m. without some kind of drug to get me going. I definitely had all of this figured wrong. I thought when I came to treatment, I'd be laying around watching television, kicking back most of the day and maybe catch a few AA meetings. I'd only been there one day and already I wanted to leave.

I got up and fixed everyone breakfast. That was probably the first time in a few years that I actually ate breakfast. My breakfast was usually some sort of powder snorted up the nose. I cleaned up the mess and then we had group therapy. In group we went around and shared some of our experiences, and tried to understand some of our common problems. I had the opportunity to listen to others and hear their problems, and also had the opportunity to meet some of the counselors.

After group they gave me the AA big book and explained the twelve-step program. We went for some exercise and then we came back for lunch. I hadn't eaten three square meals in a long time. When I went in for treatment I weighed about 130 lbs. When I came out I weighed 165. I hadn't eaten that much food in a long time. After lunch we worked on the twelve-step program some more and then we did chores and had dinner. After dinner we went to bed. It was pretty much the same routine every day.

I never did sleep real well while I was in there. When I did sleep I had terrible dreams, mostly about drugs and other weird stuff. More often than not, I just laid awake thinking. I stayed in that treatment facility for thirty-five days and had a lot of time to try and figure things out.

One person I came to respect a lot was the main counselor. His name was John and he was a recovering drug addict. Heroin had become his drug of choice and like me he had messed his life up pretty good before he finally came around. We spoke a lot and he explained some things to me about addiction; how addictions worked and how your addictions continue to grow, even when you're not using. Once you quit using, if you start again, your addiction is worse than when you left off. John told me a lot of things I didn't want to hear, but that I needed to hear. When I started filling him with BS he could see right through me.

We all loaded up one night and headed for an AA meeting in Layton. I spoke that evening for the first time and introduced myself as an alcoholic-addict. I'll never forget how I felt when I said that. Alcoholics and addicts were always weird, diseased people that slept in alleys and passed out in gutters with half empty bottles of whiskey lying next to them. When I was young I always pictured alcoholics as old people that needed to shave, that were staggering down the street with holes in their pants and had old shoes on with no shoelaces.

At the first AA meeting I had gone to a few years back, I was amazed that people could actually allow themselves to get so messed up and lose everything: their jobs, their families, their self-respect. Yet here I was, a normal looking, average, everyday person that had lost it all. I was just as bad as any alcoholic out there.

It felt good to share and tell some of my story. It also felt good to know that I wasn't alone. There were a lot of people that were in the same boat as me. When I was in treatment I started to feel that there was hope and that I wasn't a lost cause, something I hadn't felt for a long time. I started to pray again and ask our father in heaven if he would help me. I hadn't prayed for a long time. I asked him to help me get rid of some of the cravings I had; cravings to go back and use drugs, and drink. It seemed like when I prayed, my prayers were always answered. It felt good to know that there really was a God and that he cared about me.

One of the steps in AA is to believe in a power greater than yourself. Because of my religious background I always did believe in God, so it wasn't hard for me to choose God as my higher power. I hadn't felt the spirit for a long time so it felt good to pray and to feel the presence of the spirit in my life. I felt hope and I felt good inside.

I started working the twelve-step program and began to understand why I had done a lot of the things I had done. I was working with a lot of people that had some of the same problems. Some of them were in much worse shape than me. My family came to visit and I was happy to see them. When I first went into treatment, I didn't want my kids to know I was there. Now that I had been in there for a while and had cleaned up, I was ready to see them. I asked my mom if she would bring them in. When they came, I was very happy. They wanted to know why I was there and when I was getting out. I told them that their dad was very sick and that I had to stay until I got better. I love my kids more than anything I have in this world. I would do anything for any one of them.

12.

My court day was coming up and I was going to have to get out of rehab to go. As the day was getting closer I started to worry about all the things that I was going to have to face. I had two felony drug charges and two DUI's. I felt good about the progress I had made in treatment, but I really didn't know if it was going to do any good when I had to face the judge.

I arrived early at my lawyer's request. He told me that the judge I had was the worst judge I could have got. He said that if I were lucky, I would probably get off with six months in county jail. I cringed at the idea of having to spend six months locked up. To a lot of people that have spent time in prison, six months is nothing, but to me it seemed like a lifetime.

When it was my turn, I let my attorney do all of the talking. The prosecuting attorney was asking for a minimum of four years in prison. I almost had a heart attack when he said that. My attorney was good and pled my case the best he could. When the judge had finished hearing both sides, he asked me if I had anything to say for myself. I approached him and said that I was truly sorry for the things that I had done and felt that the treatment center I was currently in was doing a lot of good. I asked if I could finish treatment before I was sentenced. I also told him that I planned on getting involved in outpatient meetings and was going to do whatever it took to stay clean. He scheduled my sentencing for a later date and we left.

I went back for one more week of treatment and was released. I felt good about the time I spent in there and left feeling confident that I would be able to stay clean. About a week later, I had to go to court for sentencing. When the judge called my name, I was very nervous. I stood and my attorney stood. He approached the judge and pled my case one last time before sentencing. The judge sentenced me to three and a half years in prison. He paused for what seemed forever, and then he said, "suspended upon completion of eighteen months of supervised probation, thirty days in county jail, fines and community service."

My attorney was amazed. He told me that the judge must have been in an extremely good mood. The felony charges I had pending were reduced to first class misdemeanors. I did feel that I was let off pretty easy considering the circumstances. I had to go to county jail immediately and start my thirty-day sentence. After I had been in for a couple of days, my attorney requested work release. I was able get out during the day to work. My dad had said that he would give me a job working in his warehouse. I spent eight days in full lock up and was then granted work release. I feel very fortunate with all of the mistakes I've made, and all of the stupid things I've done, that this was the most time that I ever served in jail. I served the time I had to do and was released.

I had been in touch with a couple of my friends and had some work lined up out of town if I wanted it. I had been clean and sober for a little more than sixty days now and felt good about that. In all the time I had been using I had never been able to go more than a couple of weeks, so sixty days was an accomplishment for me.

I took the work that was offered and ended up in Roosevelt, Utah. I was sandblasting and painting again and was just very happy to be out of jail and working. Staying sober didn't last very long though. In fact, after we finished the first day of work we went back to the hotel we were staying in and everyone started drinking beer. I didn't even hesitate; I started drinking like I had never stopped. I justified it by telling myself that as long as I didn't do any drugs, I would be ok. I was able to maintain pretty well and was able to hold down the job I had for quite a while. After finishing in Roosevelt, we moved on to Elko, Nevada.

13.

I always stayed in touch with my brother Dean in Las Vegas and found out that he had started his own business. He was doing the same thing he was doing before, but this time it was for himself. He told me to keep in touch and when his business started doing well he would have me come to Vegas and go to work with him. In the meantime, my drinking started getting worse. I went from drinking a couple of beers, to four and then eight and then I would drink until I passed out. I did manage to stay away from drugs for a while.

I worked my way up to Colorado and was on a bridge crew just outside of Denver. We were painting and sandblasting bridges. I then moved on to Laramie, Wyoming. I was working in a big oil field up there, sandblasting tanks and pipe. My brother got ahold of me in my room one night and told me to move to Vegas. His business was doing better and he said I could move in with him and his family until I could afford to move out. I quit my job in Wyoming and headed for Vegas.

Living with my brother was good in the sense that I was able to quit drinking again. I went to work for his new company, Western States Trade Show Services Inc. My brother started pushing the religion thing again whenever he could. I decided this time that it wouldn't hurt to maybe give it a try, so I did make an honest effort to see if it would work for me. He got me started on reading the Book of Mormon and wanted me to go to church with him and his family. I felt so uncomfortable and out of place the first time I went. I felt like everyone was looking at me, like I was some low life. I know now that these feelings came from Satan. I was making an honest effort to make some changes come about in my life and Satan was doing everything in his power to prevent this from happening.

My brother introduced me to his bishop and I even agreed to go to an interview with him. He asked me a lot of questions and I was very honest with him. I just wasn't ready to make the kind of commitment I needed to make. I kept reading the Book of Mormon but couldn't make any sense of it. I even tried to pray about it, but it didn't seem to make any difference. I have learned since, when you have doubt it is impossible to exercise faith. Faith and doubt cannot exist at the same time. I was so filled with doubt and unbelief that I didn't have room to exercise any faith. I quit trying to understand and make any sense of what I was reading. I quit going to church with my brother and his family. The bottom line was, I just plain quit.

I had my probation transferred to Las Vegas and was still having to check in with a probation officer. Another thing that happened when I was sentenced was I lost my driving privileges for one year. My year was almost up and I could hardly wait for the day that I could drive again. Up to this point I had to rely on someone else to take me where I needed to go. I flew to Bountiful, got my license back, and picked up my car. I felt free again. Being able to drive again was a good thing. My insurance was way high, but at least I could drive. Before I got my car, I was confined to my brother's house. Now I had the freedom to go wherever I wanted. This made it possible to go hit the bars, and casinos and to fall back into my old habits. I wasn't much of a gambler yet because I hated losing money, and all of the times I had tried to gamble, I never won anything. I had been living with my brother now for almost eight months and I figured it was about time for me to find a place of my own.

I had just got my tax returns back and my brother's business was doing well enough that he was able to put me on a steady salary. It didn't take me long to find a place that I felt was suitable for what I needed. At the time I wasn't very familiar with Las Vegas and the apartment complex I moved into was in a bad section of town. I borrowed my brother's truck and drove to Utah to my mom's house and picked up all my things. The apartment I rented was only a one-bedroom, but it was good enough for me. After being there a short time, I discovered that the apartment directly above me was rented to a bunch of drug dealers. The traffic coming in and out of their apartment was non-stop. Especially on the weekends.

My apartment had a nice pool, so when I got off work, I'd load up a cooler full of beer and go there to hang out. It was nice to be on my own, but the freedom I gained allowed me to start drinking heavily again. I got to be good friends with my next-door neighbors. They were a couple, about the same age as me, with two young kids. The lady, whose name was Jodie, was very friendly and started coming over a lot to party. Jodie was a little on the wild side and used to take off and go gambling a lot. She would come over and try to get me to go with her. I knew that she was married and I really didn't want to get involved in going out with a married woman.

She came over one night with a couple of her friends and asked me if I wanted to do some coke. I hadn't done cocaine for a long time and wasn't about to get started on that again, so I told her thanks for the offer, but no thanks. She dumped a big pile on my counter and she and her friends did some and left a good amount sitting there. I guess she was just being nice and figured that maybe later I would change my mind. After she left, I stared at that pile of coke for a long time. I was drinking a few beers and the more I drank the better it looked. I finally allowed my weakness to get the best of me and I did a little. I figured that as long as I only did a little it would be all right. As I mentioned before, cocaine is a drug that is very hard to do just a little of. Once you get started you usually won't stop until it's all gone. I justified what I was doing by telling myself it was ok as long as I didn't shoot it or smoke it. So, here I was once more, walking the all too familiar dark path to destruction. The path I knew so well.

Satan is very good at what he does. He slithers himself into your life a little at a time. He is a master at deception and a very smooth, cunning operator. He knows our weaknesses better than we do. After a while, I was drinking every day, doing cocaine here and there, and I was back to partying as much as I possibly could.

My ex-wife was allowing me to see my kids again, so they would come and stay with me every summer for two or three weeks. I always enjoyed being able to spend time with my kids. My lease was coming up on the apartment I was renting and I really didn't want to stay there anymore. I found a bigger apartment on the other side of town and moved.

Jodie and her husband had bought a house and were in the process of moving. After they moved, Jodie would come over all the time, or I would go over there. They were starting to have problems in their marriage; problems that had started long before she met me. After I moved, she decided to leave her husband and needed a place to stay, so she and her two kids moved into my apartment. She ended up filing for divorce and a couple of months later it was final.

Jodie and I did love each other and had discussed the possibilities of getting married. We bought a house together and were married a couple of months later. The house we bought was nice and we decided to have a pool put in the backyard. When we were married we didn't have a big fancy wedding, we just went to one of the wedding chapels in Vegas and had immediate family come and were married. Jodie and I would probably still be married if it wasn't for all the drugs and alcohol. I have never seen a successful marriage where either person had a serious drug or alcohol problem. Drugs and alcohol are some of Satan's strongest tools he uses to destroy people's lives and to destroy marriages.

Jodie and I settled into our new lives together and got along very well for a while. We still partied a lot and had a lot of pool parties at our house. We both had connections for any drugs we needed, so we both started doing way too much cocaine. My addiction to cocaine was as bad now as it ever was. I swore up and down and promised myself over and over again, that I would never allow myself to fall back into that sewer, but I was right back where I left off. Pretty soon I was free-basing again. I would spend all night long running around the house, looking out windows, and locking myself in the bathroom. I was doing the same crazy stuff I used to do, except now it was ten times worse.

What my counselor had told me in treatment was true: your addictions to drugs and alcohol continue to grow inside of you, even when you're not using.

When you do start up again, you're worse off than when you stopped. He also told me that there are different stages of addiction. Being paranoid all the time is one of the final stages of drug addiction and is just like being insane. The absolute final stage is death. If I had ever reached that stage I wouldn't be here right now to tell this story, but I can honestly say that I walked on the edge of death several times.

I had reached a point where I hated doing cocaine. I hated what it did to me. I hated running around my house and being paranoid all night, but I just couldn't quit. No matter how hard I tried, or how many times I promised myself that I was going to quit, I just couldn't do it. Jodie and I would buy a bunch of coke, do it all night, go to work the next day and be hating life. We swore off of cocaine so many times. Whenever all the bad would wear off, we'd get some sleep and everything would go back to being normal. Then we'd go buy some more and start the cycle all over again. It was like being on a roller coaster ride that never ended.

14.

My brother's business was getting very busy. I was basically in charge of all supervision and show services at all the shows we were doing. I was in charge of coordinating all labor and making sure that all of our clientele were taken care of. I had been working the business with my brother for a few years now and was very good at what I did. I had become familiar with all aspects of the trade show industry.

I had a lot of friends that worked for us off and on, depending on how busy we were in different shows. Because of all the hours involved and the deadlines that have to be met in this industry, methamphetamine is a very popular drug among a lot of the workers involved. A good friend of mine came over to our house one night and had some meth with him. We started doing some, and by the end of the night I was amazed at the way I was reacting to it. I had done it all night and wasn't running around looking out windows

Randy Riggs

like I did when I was doing cocaine. I didn't get paranoid at all. I was amazed.

There are various forms of speed or meth or crystal meth or crank, or whatever you want to call it. I had done some meth in the past, but had never really got too involved with it. What I discovered that night, however, was an answer to a lot of the problems I had. I figured that if I quit doing cocaine and substituted meth for it, I could solve the problems I was having and get away from cocaine for good. Meth was much cheaper than cocaine was, and it didn't take near as much to do the job as coke did. Another thing I liked better about it was that you didn't have to do it every 10 or 15 minutes like you did coke. I don't believe that substituting one drug addiction for another was the answer I was looking for, but I knew I had to get off coke and this was my way of doing it. Not only that, I had just discovered another way to make a lot of money.

Almost all of the workers that I knew in this business were doing meth and I figured that if they were buying, they might as well buy it from me. It wasn't long and I was selling to a lot of people. I had 5 or 6 people that were like distributors for me. I would sell to them in quantity and they would sell to everyone else out there. In no time at all I had a profitable business going and was making ten to fifteen times as much money selling meth as I was working. The biggest problem I had now, was that when living the kind of lifestyle that Jodie and I were living, you spend all of the money you make partying, drinking and doing drugs.

It was at this time that I picked up another addiction, gambling. Just what I needed, another addiction. Why not, I lived in the gaming capitol of the world, Las Vegas. We had plenty of money, so why not try our luck. Jodie and I started getting babysitters for the kids at night and we would hit bars, nightclubs and casinos. It didn't matter. As long as they had slot machines, video poker, or some form of gambling and alcohol, we'd be there. In Las Vegas, as long as you're gambling, your drinks are free, or at least you think they're free. When you go into a place to gamble and you drop three or four hundred dollars and don't win anything, those free drinks end up costing quite a bit.

I was with Jodie in a bar gambling one night, playing 25-cent video poker, when I hit my first jackpot. I had only put about ten dollars in the machine and hit the progressive jackpot for $ 1,125.00. Hitting that jackpot that night was the worst thing that could have happened to me. I allowed my addictive nature to take over. I was hooked.

Jodie was working at Circus Circus as a change girl. A lot of times when I got off work, I would go there and sit at the bar and wait for her to get off. I hit two or three more jackpots there, and that was like adding fuel to the fire that was already burning. Jodie and I were starting to get out of control with our gambling. We would go to casinos and play blackjack, video poker, slot machines, roulette; it really didn't matter as long as we were having fun.

Between Jodie working, and my working, and the drug business, we were doing very well financially. We didn't save any of the money we were making; everything we made was going to support the lifestyle we had grown accustomed to. We had become very dependent on meth. We needed it every day just to keep going. Once your body gets used to having that kick every day, or several times a day, you have to continually feed it or your body will eventually shut down. There were times during my long addiction to meth that I would go six to eight days at a time with no sleep. When you go that long without sleep you start to get really weird. You start to hallucinate. The paranoia comes back and eventually you have to shut down and sleep.

In the summer of 1993, my ex-wife had agreed to let my son Ryan come and spend the summer with me. I took off to go get him. I made the trip back with Ryan and was very happy to have him for the whole summer. Ryan is my only son and we have a great relationship.

Jodie and I were having some serious problems, but I figured we would be able to work things out. One day, while Jodie was working, I had the day off and was drinking all day. When she got home, I was pretty drunk and we started fighting. As the night progressed things got worse. It started getting ugly and pretty soon things were getting out of control. She had called her mother to come over, and I had called my brother. When my brother arrived, he took my son and Jodie's two kids and got them away from it all. Things only got worse and I told my brother to call his brother-in-law, who was a police officer and lived close to where we lived. When he got there he saw that things had gotten out of hand. He put handcuffs on Jodie and was going to take her to jail. I told him that if he had to take someone, to take me. Jodie had never had any problems with the law and I didn't want her to have to go through that. He let both of us go but made me pack up some things and leave. I had to agree to stay away for at least 24 hours.

My son and I stayed at my brother's that night, and the next day we rented one of those apartments that you rent by the week. We stayed there for a week and started looking for an apartment that we could move into permanently. We found a nice place on the other side of town and moved in. It was a new apartment and was very nice, and it also got me away from the problems I was having with Jodie.

After we moved and settled in, my other two kids came down to spend the rest of the summer with us. In spite of all that had happened, it still ended up being one of the best summers I have ever spent with my kids.

The drug business I had put together was still going and I kept selling drugs, even with my kids being there. I always had to come up with excuses why there were so many people stopping by. I would have to come up with reasons why I had to go places and they couldn't come. By the time my kids left that summer, my addiction to meth and the business I had built was bigger than ever.

15.

I would get off work at Western States and run all over Las Vegas selling drugs. Sometimes I would be out all night making deliveries and collecting money that people owed me. I was making so much money it was insane. This is about the time that my gambling started getting even more out of control. I went over to a bar one day at lunch when a show was going on at the convention center. I had a lot of money and playing 25-cent video poker was getting boring, so I started playing dollars. I had put one hundred dollars in one machine and hadn't won anything. I bought another hundred-dollar rack. I had only put about another twenty dollars in when I hit a royal flush for $ 4700.00. I was totally stunned. I had never in my life won that much money. The problem is, when you win $ 1200.00 or more, you have to sign a tax form and it goes to the IRS. Hitting that jackpot sent me into a gambling frenzy.

Every spare minute I had, I was in the bars or casinos gambling. I spent so much money gambling it was ridiculous. When people needed drugs, instead of going to their houses, or having them come to mine, I would have them meet me at casinos or bars. All the money I was making from selling drugs was going into the machines. I was making and spending a fortune. The more money I made, the more money I gambled. I was on the gambling, drugs, and drinking roller coaster ride from hell, or I should say to hell because that is exactly where all of this was taking me.

Pretty soon most of the meth that was going around the Las Vegas Convention Center during set-up and takedown of shows, was coming from me. I had stepped up my business a lot and had several people out there that were selling for me. I had so much going on that I started making runs to California. I was picking up drugs from several different sources in California and ended up connecting with some of the Mexican Cartel. I was picking up in large quantities and bringing it all back to Vegas. The demand was unreal. At times, I'd bring back two or three pounds and it would be gone as soon as I got back. I'd have to turn around and go back to get more.

In 1995 things were getting crazier than they had ever been. I met a girl named Suzanne, who had a small business of her own and needed a supplier. I don't really remember all of the details, but she didn't have a place to live and ended up moving into my apartment. I wasn't divorced from Jodie yet and was still seeing her and trying to figure out if we could salvage our marriage. When she found out about Suzanne, she immediately filed for divorce.

My performance at work was getting bad. My whole life was a confused mess. I was so busy taking care of the drug business I hardly ever slept. I had gone from snorting meth to smoking it which, once again, takes twice as much and messes you up ten times worse. I would be talking to my brother in his office and fall asleep talking to him. Several times he would walk into my office and I'd be sitting at my desk, snoring away. He warned me several times that if I didn't straighten up, I was going to be looking for another job. I know if I hadn't been his brother, he would have let me go long before he did.

One of our big shows was going on and he was depending on me being there first thing in the morning to start dismantling it. I didn't show up and he came to my apartment. When I woke up to answer the door, he totally went off. I thought for sure that he was going to fire me, but he didn't. He gave me another warning and told me I had better straighten up. I didn't straighten up, I only got worse. I was still selling and smoking meth and drinking and gambling.

The next show we had come in was the biggest show that we did. We had major work to do on it and my brother was relying heavily on me. I guess this was the straw that broke the camel's back. When the show was running, he had his office manager call me at home and fire me. It must have been too hard for him to do, so he had her do it. I had been working for

Western States Trade Show Services for ten years and now it was over. The sad thing about it was, I really didn't care. I was so busy doing other things that work was getting in the way. Besides, I was making ten times as much money selling drugs, as I ever did working.

I went to the office and turned in my cell phone, credit cards, pager, and everything else I had that belonged to Western States, and left. My brother wasn't there when I came, so I just left him a nasty letter. I told him in that letter, that as far as I was concerned he wasn't my brother anymore and I didn't care if I ever saw him again. Dean and I have always been close and still are. He hadn't done anything wrong, yet I tried to blame him for everything that was going wrong in my life.

Now that I wasn't working at Western States, I had the freedom to do anything I wanted. I went almost a full year before I spoke with my brother again. Suzanne had gotten as bad with drugs and gambling as I had, and we were both on a one-way ride to hell. I caught Suzanne shooting drugs in her arm one day and told her if I caught her again I would throw her out of my apartment. The biggest reason I told her I didn't want her doing it that way, is because I knew if I was around her doing it for very long, pretty soon I'd be doing it too. I caught her three more times and didn't throw her out, which was a big mistake. Just as I figured, it was only a matter of time and I was shooting drugs in my arm again.

I was so messed up in my life at this point; I couldn't believe that I was back in the same boat I'd been in so many times before. Deep down I knew that I was headed for disaster. I knew that if I kept going the way I was, it could only end badly. Once again, I just didn't care. I had fought hard before to avoid heading down the road I was now traveling. I knew exactly where it would end, but I kept on doing the things that would destroy my life. I was gambling like crazy, and I thought that I had Vegas all figured out.

I hit a lucky streak about this time that was unbelievable. I was winning and hitting jackpots wherever I went. I was hitting four thousand dollar royal flushes on dollar machines everywhere. One night I went to a bar with Suzanne and hit a royal flush for four thousand dollars. They paid me with a check. I went to the Palace Station to cash it and started playing five-dollar video poker. I hit another royal flush on a five-dollar machine and won twenty thousand dollars. After I collected the money for that, we went back to the same bar we started in and I won another four thousand dollars. Altogether that night, I had won twenty-eight thousand dollars. I couldn't believe what was happening.

A couple weeks later, Suzanne hit a jackpot at the MGM for twenty-seven thousand dollars. We were sitting in my apartment one night and counted the money we had. I counted sixty thousand dollars in cash. We weren't even half way through 1995 and I had already signed for about $ 150,000. We also had over three pounds of meth on hand, ready to sell. I really did think that I had it all figured out. Who needed to work when you could go out and win money this easy and sell drugs and make the kind of money I was making. It all came so fast and easy, it was unreal.

Suzanne and I paid up a two-year lease on a brand new, 1995 forty-year anniversary addition Thunderbird. The car was fully loaded and was beautiful. We bought nice clothes, jewelry and just about anything else we wanted. We were living the highlife, and nothing could get in our way. Or so we thought. On Thanksgiving weekend of that same year, I was kicked out of my apartment, I was dead broke, and I was homeless.

16.

One night, a friend of mine came over after he had picked up a how-to book on manufacturing meth. I was fascinated by what I was reading and thought that it might be an easy thing to do. All I needed was the necessary equipment and a way to get the chemicals needed to do it. It amazes me that a person can go to a bookstore, or get on the Internet and get a detailed recipe on how to manufacture meth. I studied this book for hours and figured it didn't sound that difficult, so I set out to find the things I needed.

I'm not going to get into detail on how I manufactured meth. I'm only going to say that it took a long time and it was a lot harder than I had figured it would be. I blew up a couple kitchens and caught myself on fire two or three times, before I finally figured it out. Suzanne tried more than once to get me to give it up. I've always been very stubborn and told her I would figure it out, or die trying. The latter almost happened several times. I finally did figure it out and was making some of the highest quality meth in Vegas.

We were homeless and living in the Thunderbird we had bought, so finding a place to set up a lab was always a problem. I had won so much money gambling in various hotels that I started using my comps and was setting up labs in hotels. On my MGM gambling card alone I had 7 million points. I would go in and get rooms comped, bring all the stuff up to the room and make a batch or two. I did this in hotel rooms all over Las Vegas. I couldn't keep up with the demand. As soon as I would make a batch, I had several people that were waiting and I would sell it faster than I could make it. The stupid thing was that every time I'd sell a good amount and make some money, Suzanne and I would go to the casino and lose it all gambling.

One thing that stands out in my mind was the evil presence I felt when I was making meth. It was a presence that would send chills up and down your spine. One night we were in the Hacienda Hotel. It was late and Suzanne was asleep. I was cooking up a batch and I was watching the chemicals react in the flask. I felt a presence that was so strong it scared me half to death. I had felt this before and knew that as I was sitting there in that room, Satan himself was sitting there right next to me. After all it was his poison that I was mixing. I was so scared, I woke Suzanne up and she felt it too. As scary as it was, it still wasn't enough to make me quit.

On another night we were in a motel on south Las Vegas Blvd. We had been in the room all that day cooking meth and had a few people drop by. We were sitting there watching TV when the windows came crashing in and the door came flying across the room. Someone had called the cops. There were cops everywhere. They were all dressed in army fatigues and had oxygen masks on and full combat gear, with automatic weapons. It was unreal. They forced us out of the room and threw us face down on the asphalt, handcuffed us and tore the room apart looking for drugs. They found all the chemicals, all the glassware and everything else they needed to convict us of drug manufacturing. They took us to Clark County Detention Center and booked us in.

The place was so overcrowded that they let us out the next morning. When we were released, we called some friends to pick us up and they gave us a ride to the motel to get our car. We were given a phone number and had to check in weekly, so the cops would know where we were at all times. They would also let us know when we had to go to court. If we failed to check in, they would issue warrants for our arrests.

This was definitely some serious trouble we had gotten ourselves into. We stayed with a friend out in South Las Vegas for a couple of days. We then got in our car and took off. We had no jobs, no money, no home, and no life. I had never been this low. I couldn't believe that I had allowed myself to become what I was. Suzanne and I were going into grocery stores and stealing food, stealing cigarettes, and stealing booze. I couldn't believe that all this was going on in my life. I hadn't stolen anything in years and here I was, stealing to survive. Suzanne had tried several times to get me to call someone in my family for help. My brother lived in Vegas and my dad lived in St. George and I had plenty of people that would have helped, but I didn't want to call any of them. I figured that this time I had got myself into this mess and it was going to have to be me that got myself out of it.

We finally got ahold of some friends that were willing to put up the money we needed to get back into business and get the things we needed to start making meth again. After all that had happened, you would think that it would have scared me into turning my life around, but I didn't know what else to do, or who to turn to. At this time, cooking meth and selling it was all I knew how to do.

I had left Suzanne in a room one day sleeping and went to make a delivery. I was over at some friends' house and ended up staying for a while to visit. When I came out of their house a little later my car had been stolen. I was depending on that car as my only means to get around Las Vegas, and relying on it to sleep in half the time, and now it was gone. I called Suzanne and she was totally losing it. I called the cops and reported it stolen. I also informed the insurance company that it had been stolen. When we bought the car, and had all that money, we managed to pay up an insurance policy on the car for about a year. We ended up staying with some friends that lived over in the area where my car was stolen. We stayed there for about a week and kind of wore out our welcome. We had to move along, but had no way of going anywhere.

I called the Frontier Hotel and asked them if I had enough points on my card to get a room for a few nights. They said I did, so we grabbed what belongings we had and started to walk over to the strip. I'll never forget that night for the rest of my life. It was about midnight and we were walking down Spring Mountain Road toward the Las Vegas strip. We were carrying some clothes that we had in garbage bags. Here we were, in the brightest city in the world and never in my life had I felt so alone and so dark. I felt totally empty; I had never been as low as I was now. I didn't know what I was going to do or how I was going to get myself out of this one.

We finally made it to the Frontier Hotel and checked in. When they comp you rooms, they expect you to gamble with the card they give you. We had no money and no way to gamble, so we just stayed in the room and slept. I seriously wanted to go to sleep and never wake up.

Before our car had been stolen, we had managed to make a little extra money to buy some Christmas presents for my kids. Christmas was only a couple of days away at the time. Suzanne and I had planned on making a trip to Salt Lake to see my kids and spend some time with them. I was waking up in a hotel room in Las Vegas instead.

This was the loneliest Christmas I had ever experienced. I had to call my kids and at least wish them a Merry Christmas. I still had my calling card from Western States and used it to call them. They were all worried about me because I hadn't talked with them for so long. I told them what had happened and that my car had been stolen with all of their presents in it. I know they probably thought that I made it all up, but it really was the truth. My youngest daughter Coco wouldn't even talk to me. I never felt worse in my life than I did that day. My own kids didn't have any respect for me. They knew what was going on in my life and I guess they just didn't know what to think. I finally did talk to Coco and she was in tears. I felt so bad that I didn't know what to say. Words could never even begin to explain what I felt that day as I was talking to my kids. This was definitely as low and empty as anyone could possibly be in life. After hanging up the phone, I cried for a long time.

I called my mom a little while later and talked to her for awhile. I just wanted her to know I was ok and that everything was all right, even though it wasn't. She begged me to come home and told me that I could stay with her until I got my feet back on the ground. I assured her that I would be ok and she told me that she loved me and that was about it. Next, I called my dad to let him know that I was all right and to wish him and Dionne, my step-mom, a Merry Christmas. One of the first things he said to me was that he didn't have any money he could send me. I was totally in shock because I wasn't even thinking about asking him for money, but what could I expect him to say. I was just like the bums you see on the street. I didn't have a job, I was homeless and I wasn't any better off than any street scum alcoholic that you see crawling out of an alley looking for some kind of a handout. I just assured him that I was ok and wished them a Merry Christmas and that was that.

It was that Christmas day that I finally started thinking that I needed to do something different in my life. If I was ever going to have some kind of a normal life, or win back the respect I wanted so badly from my kids, I was going to have to do something to change things. The biggest problem was I didn't know how to do it, or whom I could turn to. Here I was, 38 years old and had nothing to show for anything.

We checked out of the Frontier Hotel and I know that they were glad to see us go. When you're gambling all the time like I was, they roll out the red carpet and give you anything you want. I had standing comp tickets to all the shows at Caesars Palace every month. I could get rooms at almost any hotel on the strip and free dinners at some of the best restaurants in Las Vegas. But once you stop gambling, they don't even remember your name.

I got ahold of our insurance company and they said that if our car wasn't found within a couple of weeks they were going to give us a check for around $ 8,000.00. I was hoping at this point that they wouldn't find the car, because I really could have used the money instead. As messed up as I was, I probably would have done something stupid and gambled it anyway. They found our car in the Palace Station parking lot. When we went to get the car, it was all right, but everything we had in it was gone; all the clothes we had bought and all the Christmas presents for my kids. Everything was taken, except one coat I had bought for my oldest daughter Jamie.

One thing I had come to realize was that everything I had purchased or acquired while I was selling drugs or gambling had either been stolen or something happened to it. All of the clothes I had bought for Suzanne and myself had been stolen. The car we purchased had done nothing but given us problems; it was like some kind of bad luck curse had been put on everything we owned.

We were happy to get our car back. At least now we had a place to sleep. A lot of times when we were homeless and had nowhere to go, we would just pull into a store parking lot, or a Casino parking lot, lay the seats back and go to sleep. The Thunderbird we had was more comfortable than a lot of the hotels we stayed in. It sure was a lot better than not having anything at all.

Once we were back in our car we didn't waste time. We needed money fast, so again we did the only thing we knew. We raised the money we needed to get the glassware, scrounged up enough money to get a room, and went right back to doing what we did best: making and selling meth. At this point, fast money was all I knew. I hadn't worked an honest job, or made an honest buck for at least eight months.

We were in one of those rent-by-the-week apartments again and had all the chemicals and equipment needed to make a big batch of meth. I started everything going and for some reason, something wasn't right. As soon as it started cooking, it was reacting differently than I had ever seen. I don't know if I had put wrong chemical amounts in, or what the deal was, but it was reacting violently. The chemicals used to manufacture meth are extremely dangerous. If you don't know what you are doing it can be deadly. Once again, I felt the evil presence I always felt when I was doing Satan's work. Something went totally wrong with this batch and as I was standing over it, trying to figure out what to do, it blew up. The chemicals were everywhere. When the mixture had blown up, it went all over the walls. I was covered and there was smoke everywhere. It sounded like a stick of dynamite had gone off and I figured any moment there would be cops everywhere. A sharp piece of glass had shot straight into my stomach. I didn't dare pull it out until we got out of there. I was afraid if I did pull it out I would bleed to death.

We hurried out of there, got in the car and rushed over to a friend's house that wasn't far away. When we arrived at her house, I headed straight for the shower. I hurried and rinsed everything off and covered myself with baking soda to neutralize the acid that was burning up my skin. I pulled the piece of glass out of my stomach and blood was oozing out all over the place. It was a serious enough injury that I should have gone to the hospital for emergency treatment. I knew that I definitely needed stitches. I wasn't about to do that because they would have wanted ID at the hospital and probably would have called the police. Suzanne went to the store and bought all kinds of first aid supplies and some butterfly bandages. We bandaged everything up and everything seemed to be all right. We were very reluctant to go back to the apartment, but we knew we had to go and see what the damages were. To our surprise, no one had been there and nobody had reported anything.

As we walked into that room, I couldn't believe the dark feeling that was present. I felt as if I was walking into the scene of a homicide. There was red chemical everywhere. The bathroom I had set everything up in was covered with the poison I was making. The smell was almost unbearable, the evil presence was scary.

We went to the hardware store and bought all the supplies we needed to clean up the mess. We bought paint and primer and all kinds of cleaning supplies. We scrubbed the walls down the best we could and rolled a coat of white primer to cover all the red from the chemicals. No matter what we did, the red kept bleeding through. We would put a coat on and let it dry, and another coat, but no matter how many times we did it, it still kept bleeding through. We ended up putting about six coats of primer and paint on and sprayed Lysol disinfectant to cover the smell of meth that was so strong in the room. The smell never did go away.

We went to bed that night and started again in the morning. We worked all day and into the night to clean up the mess we had made. It was early evening when someone knocked on the door. I opened the door and there were cops everywhere. Someone that was at our friend's house when we went over to get cleaned up had called the police and told them where we were and what was going on. We had enough meth in that apartment to put us away for a long time. We were arrested, handcuffed, and taken away to jail again. They searched my car and found chemicals and other paraphernalia. They impounded the car and I never saw it again.

This time I knew I was in deep. I didn't see anyway at all that I was going to get out of this without serving time in prison. They had me for felony possession with intent to sell, and two counts of felony manufacturing meth. When they arrested us and booked us into county jail, they released us again without having to put up bail. When we were released, we had no way of getting anywhere because our car was gone.

It was about 1a.m. and I didn't really know anyone that we could call. We walked up the street to the bus station and lay down on the lawn. I was so tired all I wanted to do was sleep. I found a comfortable spot on the grass and closed my eyes. The next thing I knew it was morning and the sun shining in my face woke me up. Suzanne and I were surrounded by a lot of other people who were also sleeping there. I didn't have any idea when we fell asleep, that this was where a lot of the homeless people in Las Vegas slept. We were right in the middle of about twenty to thirty homeless bums, all sound asleep. I kept thinking, "This must be a bad dream and I'm going to wake up at anytime." My whole life was one bad nightmare. Nothing I could have done in my life could have prepared me for what I was now facing. I had just been arrested again, I didn't have a home, I didn't have a job; my life was a total confused, mixed up mess. I didn't know what to do or where to go. To top it all off, here we were sleeping in the middle of a bunch of bums. I looked at these people and thought, "What am I doing here. I don't belong here." The sad thing was, I was no better than any of these bums that were lying next to me. If anything, they were probably in better shape than I was, and I'm sure that I didn't look any better than any of them.

17.

We managed to scrounge up enough money to get on the bus and head for south Las Vegas Blvd. We had a friend that owned a condo out that way and we were going to see if she would let us stay there for a couple of days. When we arrived at her place she was getting ready to go out of town for a couple of weeks. She told us that we were welcome to stay there until she got back. We were both so tired we couldn't even function. We had run out of meth and our bodies were ready to completely shut down.

We ended up staying in that condo for almost three weeks. In that time, all we were able to do was sleep. We woke up every now and then, grabbed something to eat, and went right back to sleep. When I finally got to where I could function, I decided that I really did need to make some changes in my life. I couldn't do this anymore. I was sick of doing drugs. I was tired of always having to look over my shoulder everywhere I went. I was sick of all my so-called friends. I was sick of drinking. I couldn't believe it, but I truly was sick of everything. Looking up at the ceiling for a long time I thought, "God, I really don't know if you are there or not, but if you are I really and truly need you to help me." For the first time in my life I really did mean what I said. I always knew that there was a God, but this time, unlike many times before, I really was serious and willing to do whatever it took to change my life.

It was almost exactly three weeks before I had enough energy to get up and walk around. I started taking vitamins. My body was so used to doing meth it just didn't know how to function without it. It was almost like I had to train my whole system all over again to work without chemicals.

We decided that it was time to move on, so we packed up what we had and left. We had another friend, who lived in the same complex, who owed us some money from a drug deal about a month earlier. We knocked on his door and he invited us in. He didn't have any money, but offered to let us stay there for however long we needed. I started to pray every day and was asking for help any way I could get it. I really did feel for the first time in a long time that my prayers were being heard.

I finally broke down and called my mom in Bountiful. She was worried about me because she hadn't heard from me in a long time. She still wanted me to come and stay with her until I could get my life together. I told her not to worry and that I would be in touch with her. I called my brother Dean and told him I would stop by and see him. Suzanne was starting to ask me a lot of questions about my religion. I answered them the best I could, but told her she would have to talk to my brother. He knew a lot more about it than I did.

We ended up having him come and get us one night and we went to his house to visit. I hadn't seen my brother in almost a year. He was as glad to see me, as I was to see him. We talked for a long time. We talked about my kids and Dean told me that he had seen them not to long ago and that I needed to go back to Salt Lake to see them. He told me that all of my kids had lost respect in me, especially Coco. I sat there at my brother's house and cried. It felt good to just cry and let it all out. I hadn't done that for a long time and I was sick about my whole life. Suzanne also had a lot of questions about our religion, which Dean was able to answer for her.

We stayed at our friend's house for about another week or so and I decided that if I was going to straighten up, I really needed to get away from Vegas for a while. Maybe for good. I called my mom again and she told me that she had spoken with my friend Kim and he had a job for me in Salt Lake if I wanted it. I told her that I had decided to come to Utah for a while until I could figure out what I was going to do. I don't remember how we were able to get the money, but we rented a U-Haul truck and loaded everything we had in storage and headed for Utah.

On our way to Utah, Suzanne was asking more questions about the church. She asked me if I believed in our church. I told her that I had quit going at such a young age, that I really didn't know enough about it. I did tell her that I felt deep inside that it was true; I just had a hard time living the way that people in our church lived. Living life without drugs or alcohol was beyond my comprehension. How could one have fun in life without them?

My mom called the missionaries to come over and teach Suzanne about our religion. When they came over, they invited me to sit in with them. I told them that they could teach Suzanne, but it was way to late for me and there wasn't any point in them wasting their time on me. They asked me a lot of questions that night. I told them a little bit of what I had been through. I didn't tell them a lot because my mom was there and I didn't want to upset her. There were a lot of details that she just didn't need to know at this time.

They explained the atonement to me and got into a little bit of detail about Christ and what his mission here on the earth was all about. I listened in amazement because I really never did understand what the atonement was all about. They told me that no matter how bad the things I had done were, if I followed the steps of repentance, I could be forgiven. It all sounded good to me, but I wasn't sure I was ready to make that kind of commitment yet. They also told me that if I was serious about making changes in my life, that this was where I was going to have to start.

Since I was still a member of the church, they were going to set up an appointment with the bishop for me. I did a lot of thinking that night and did want to change my life. I had told God and myself that night in Vegas, that I was ready and willing to do whatever it took to make the necessary changes.

I was a little nervous about going to talk to the bishop, but I felt that it was something I needed to do. I went in not really knowing what to expect. I figured that after I told him all the things I had done, he was probably going to excommunicate me from the church. I went in and sat down and he started asking me a lot of questions. I was very honest with him and told him everything. I went all the way back to when it first started and confessed everything to him. I felt bad about all the terrible things I had done in my life, but it felt good to get it all out. It was a big relief, almost like someone had taken 500 lbs. of weight off of my shoulders.

The bishop was very kind and understanding. He told me that he felt I didn't really have a testimony of the gospel, so he wasn't going to excommunicate me from the church. I needed to start going to church again and start studying and learning about the gospel. He assured me that I hadn't done anything that I couldn't be forgiven for.

He asked me if I was still drinking. I told him that I had a couple of beers earlier that day but I was planning on giving it up soon. He asked me to make a commitment right there and then that I would never drink again. I sat there for a long time and didn't know if I was prepared to make that kind of a commitment yet. He spoke before I did and told me if I didn't think I could do it, to not make the commitment. He also told me if I was serious about changing my life, I needed to start somewhere and this was a good place to start. I had already pretty much sworn off drugs, but giving up my beer was a big step. I looked up at the bishop and told him that I would never take another drink as long as I lived, and I meant it. I told him that I was still smoking cigarettes. He told me not to worry about that for right now. He said, "I don't want you to overwhelm yourself. You will give that up when you feel you're ready." I walked out of the bishop's office that night with a whole new attitude. I felt like I had something to live for. I felt hope for the first time in a long time.

I now knew more than I had ever known before about the atonement of Jesus Christ. I know that when Christ went into the Garden of Gethsemane, he went in there for me. I know that a lot of his suffering was for me. All of a sudden I had a strong desire to learn. I wanted to make up for lost time and learn everything I could about our church. I wanted a testimony of my own that would leave me no doubt, whatsoever, that all of this religion stuff was for real.

18.

The story I have told of my life to this point has been very dark and dreary. I had made so many mistakes and had witnessed so much evil over the years. I had a strong testimony of Satan because I had served him and his purposes for so long. I was one of his best servants and didn't even really know that I was. I watched people ruin their lives over the drugs that I was selling. I not only watched, I helped them along the way. I literally helped Satan with his designs to destroy lives, marriages, and families. I helped people to lose their self-respect. I felt terrible for the things I had done.

The first part of my story has been tough for me to talk about, or to remember. It has been therapy for me to reflect back on all of it. There are so many war stories, and so many other things I have left out because I was asked to try and keep it short. To include all of it would take a full-length novel.

Now, after twenty-five years of darkness, I could finally turn it all around and see light at the end of the tunnel. I finally get to talk about the good things. I can tell you how the Gospel of Jesus Christ has been so instrumental in making it possible for me to walk away from the life I once lived and start over. I think that the turning point in my life was the night that I walked out of the bishop's office. I had a spiritual awakening that was incredible. I was like a starved man being fed for the first time. I wanted knowledge.

I still had an empty void in my soul, only now I was beginning to fill it with spiritual things. Instead of filling that void with alcohol, or shooting drugs into my veins, or cooking meth, I was reading books, spiritual books. I was praying, asking God to help me to understand the things that I was reading. I prayed every morning and every night and sometimes three or four times during the day. I wanted so badly to learn all the things I could have learned if I hadn't started living the way I did. I asked the Lord to help me make up for lost time. I asked our Heavenly Father to help me to understand the things I was reading in the Book of Mormon and how I could apply these principles to my own life, and he did. It was amazing the things that I was learning. I was reading books written by the Prophets, the leaders of our church, both past and present. I read some of them two or three times.

I wanted to learn about Joseph Smith, so I read the Work and The Glory Series, The Teachings of Joseph Smith, Joseph Smith: The Choice Seer. I wanted to learn more about Christ, so I read Jesus The Christ, Believing Christ, The Infinite Atonement. If I had questions I would read them again. There were times when I stayed up all night reading. Sometimes I was so into what I was reading that I couldn't stop until I was done with the book. I was amazed at the knowledge that could be gained just by reading and praying, and seeking diligently to know.

If I had questions or was struggling with something, I would fast and pray. I always received answers when I did this. For the first time ever, I read the Book of Mormon from cover to cover and actually understood what I read. When I first started going to church, I felt completely out of place. But now I could go and participate in class discussions because I knew what they were talking about. It was so awesome the things that I was learning. I felt like no matter how much I read or how much I learned it was never enough.

I wanted a testimony of my own, so after I read the Book Of Mormon I tried the promise that Moroni extends to everyone that desires to know. "And when ye shall read these things, I would exhort you that ye would ask God, the Eternal Father, in the name of Christ, if these things are not true; and if ye shall ask with a sincere heart, with real intent, having faith in Christ, he will manifest the truth of it unto you, by the power of the Holy Ghost." (Moroni: 10:4) I read this scripture over and over and decided to try it. I prayed and fasted and asked for a manifestation to come to me. Nothing happened. So I read the Book of

Mormon again and fasted and prayed and again nothing happened. I was determined that if I was persistent that I would receive the answer I was looking for. I guess that I was expecting Moroni to appear to me in a beam of light like he did to Joseph Smith, but that never happened.

I continued to read the scriptures and all of the other books I was reading. One night I was praying silently in my room before I went to bed and I said, "Heavenly Father, I know with all my heart that the Book of Mormon is true. I know that this truly is the gospel of Jesus Christ and I know that Joseph Smith restored this gospel by and through the power given to him by you. Would you please give me the manifestation that I have sought for so long? Amen." After I said this prayer I realized what I had just said. I was telling our Father in Heaven that I knew the Book of Mormon was true. I knew this gospel was the true gospel of Jesus Christ. In other words I was bearing my testimony to God and telling him what I truly knew in my heart. The spirit came over me so strong that I knew at that time, I had had a testimony of all of this for a long time, I just didn't realize it. I believe that deep down I always knew.

I continued to study and to learn as much as I possibly could as I still do to this day. One thing I have found that has to be a regular routine for me is to always pray, always read, and go to all of my meetings.

The job I took with my friend Kim didn't last. I managed to find some friends in Salt Lake that backed me in starting a business doing the same thing I had been doing in Vegas; setting up and taking down exhibits in tradeshows.

Suzanne and I moved out of my mom's house and were able to get into an apartment in Salt Lake. We had the missionaries come over and they continued to teach Suzanne. She was learning a lot and wanted to be baptized. We had both come a long way from the life we were living in Vegas, but still had a long way to go. There were also drug charges pending in Las Vegas that we were going to have to face.

In July of that summer, I decided that I didn't want to smoke any more. I tried a couple of times to quit cold turkey but couldn't seem to do it. I finally decided to try the patch. The patch was a six-week program and you had to buy a box of patches every week. After three weeks, I decided I couldn't afford to buy any more patches, so I figured if I had gone three weeks, I could quit for good. Out of all the addictions I gave up, smoking was the hardest.

The day finally came and Suzanne was going to be baptized into our church. My brother drove down from Las Vegas to do the baptism and we all met at the church on a Saturday. The baptism was one of the most spiritual experiences I had ever witnessed. Suzanne and I became very active in our ward in Salt Lake. We both had some spiritual experiences that were amazing.

The day finally came for our first court arraignment. We made the trip to Las Vegas and ended up staying at my brother's house. Suzanne and I had enjoyed some amazing experiences and I figured that we were both strong enough to endure the temptations that I knew we would eventually be facing. There was a big automotive show going on at the same time we were going to Vegas, so I figured it would be a good opportunity for us to make a little extra money.

Suzanne had reached a level of spirituality after her baptism that was incredible. I was envious of her and wanted to have the spirit as strong as she did. I know to this day that Suzanne had been given a testimony. She knew in her heart and soul that the choices she had made to join the church and be baptized a member were the right choices. She was very blessed for making those decisions. I witnessed a total change come over Suzanne. She had a certain glow about her that was an amazing thing to see.

Unfortunately, there are two strong forces in this world, one is good, and one is evil. Suzanne had witnessed the good on more than one occasion and chose to become a part of that good. When one makes decisions in their life to change for the better, Satan and his dark angels will stop at nothing and work double time to mess that up. He worked very hard on both of us. That first trip we made to Vegas was hard. I ran into so many of my old friends it was unreal. The temptations were everywhere.

I was working in the convention center one day when one of my friends pulled up on a fork lift and asked me if I needed something to pick me up. Without me answering, he threw me a bag of meth and told me to go ahead and help myself. The temptation was strong but I was able to resist.

Later that evening when I was on my way back from work, I stopped at a 7-11 store to buy a drink and ran into another friend I hadn't seen in a long time. He recognized me and wanted to know if I had anything. I told him that I was clean and didn't have any. He told me that he was doing a drug deal in the store and wanted me to wait for him outside and when he was done we could go somewhere and get high. I walked out of the store, jumped in my truck and took off as fast as I could go. This guy had just recently been released from prison and was still on parole. There were several more times on that trip that I was faced with similar temptations. Satan was hot on my heels doing everything in his power to lure me back. I was able to stay focused and didn't allow myself to fall into his traps.

Suzanne wasn't as fortunate. She borrowed the truck one night and told me she had an errand to run. I didn't see her for three days. When I finally tracked her down she was a mess. She had chased down some old friends and was on a three-day binge. She had crawled right back into the sewer that we worked so hard to get out of. She missed her first court arraignment. The hardest part of it was the fact that she had to start all over again.

When we got back to Salt Lake, she went in and told the bishop what had happened. I don't think anyone was more upset than Suzanne. She managed to stay straight for a while but every time we had to go to Vegas, she always seemed to fall back onto that dreary path of darkness that we fought so hard to get away from. Suzanne went back to her old ways. I didn't know what I was going to do about my situation with her. I decided to fast and pray about it. I had a very strong impression that we needed to go our separate ways. She returned to doing all the things we had both given up. I knew then that I had made the right decision. I have spoken with her a few times over the past few years. She has been in and out of rehab centers, jails, boot camps, and other places. Things never get better in your life when you make the wrong choices. All I know is that Suzanne witnessed miraculous things that will always be with her. The spirit will always work on Suzanne and hopefully some day she'll be back.

19.

After I returned to Salt Lake, I asked the bishop if I could get my patriarchal blessing. I was given a recommend and set up a meeting with our Stake Patriarch. I was given some incredible blessings and promises. It was a great experience.

The business I had started in Salt Lake was doing ok as long as there were shows, but the shows were few and far between. I wasn't making enough money to get by and keep up with all that I had going on, so I made the decision to pack up and move back to Las Vegas. I didn't have a lot of money but I had enough to get into an apartment and enough faith to believe that if I stayed clean, went to all my church meetings, continued to study the gospel and prayed every day, everything would be all right.

I had to finish up the court stuff, which had me very nervous. I did a lot of praying about it and

promised the lord that if he would help to keep me
from going to prison, I would spend the rest of my life
doing what he wanted me to do, instead of doing things
my way. The judge was very fair and my prayers were
answered. I didn't end up going to prison. The
prosecutor did everything in his power to get me
locked up for nine years with no eligibility for parole
in less than four years. The judge ended up sentencing
me to nine years, suspended, with three years of
supervised probation, drug and alcohol counseling,
what seemed like an endless amount of community
service, and some fines. I did get convicted of two
felonies, so I have that on my record. I had a long road
to walk before I would ever be free of all of this, but I
knew that as long as I stayed clean, I would be able to
accomplish anything I set out to do.

I settled into a nice one-bedroom apartment. I
found out what ward I was in with the church and
started to go to all of my meetings. I still studied the
scriptures and read all the books I could find that had
to do with church doctrine. The deeper and more
complicated the books were, the better I liked them.
Once you make a decision to change your life, it's a
must that you change everything about your life. The
time that I used to spend drinking, gambling, doing
drugs, and just plain wasting my life away, I now
replaced with productive things like working out,
reading spiritual books, studying the gospel, working,
and learning.

After three long years of supervised probation,
what seemed like thousands of hours of community

service, extensive drug and alcohol counseling, AA meetings, fines, and a lot of other things, I was finally released from probation. One of the greatest things I now have is peace, knowing that I don't have to look over my shoulder everywhere I go. I have paid the price to society for the wrongs I committed. I'm still paying for a lot of the stupid things I did, but one by one, I'm able to put my past mistakes behind me.

My brother and I started another business that did well and provided a way for me to be able to buy a nice home, drive a decent car and be able to have enough for all my needs. I was able to dig myself out of a deep, dark hole that I never thought I would be able to climb out of. My life is still not perfect, but whose is? The Lord has blessed my life in so many ways; there is no way I could ever repay Him for all that He has done for me.

20.

I found out later, that our church sponsors a substance abuse program, which is overseen and run through the priesthood. This program was developed for people just like me who struggle with addictions. It is based on and follows the twelve-step program from Alcoholics Anonymous. I started facilitating meetings twice a week. I know for sure that my life has been saved by God and by his son Jesus Christ. If it weren't for the Lord's atonement, none of this would have been possible. Never in a million years did I ever believe that there was hope for a person who had done all of the things that I had done.

Early in my recovery, I struggled hard with cravings and overwhelming desires to drink, to use drugs, to cook meth. These cravings were sometimes more than I could bear. I was reading my scriptures one night and came across one that jumped out of the page at me. It can be found in Mormon 9:21.

"Behold, I say unto you that who so believeth in Christ, doubting nothing, whatsoever he shall ask the Father in the name of Christ it shall be granted him; and this promise is unto all, even all the ends of the earth."

I decided that asking to have these cravings and desires taken from me was a blessing that would be granted to me if I had enough faith and would simply ask. I fasted and prayed and asked to have these cravings removed once and for all. These desires and cravings were taken away. To this day, I still have no desire to go back to the life I once lived. When I went in to have my patriarchal blessing, I was told, "You will never have a desire to remove your hand from the plow and look backward." This was a blessing given to me from above. It doesn't mean that the temptations are gone; I don't believe there are many days that go by where Satan doesn't do everything in his power to try and get me back. I will say that having the cravings and desires taken away makes it a lot easier to stay clean.

If there is anyone out there that struggles with these same cravings as I once did, I promise you by the authority of the priesthood I now hold, if you ask as I did with a sincere heart and with faith in Christ, He will remove these desires from you, just as He did for me.

Another thing I wanted shortly after I moved back to Vegas was to have the Melchezidek priesthood conferred upon me, and be ordained an elder. I spoke with my bishop about it and set a goal to do whatever it took to receive this blessing. My bishop worked close with me and on my 42nd birthday, my brother Dean ordained me an elder. Next, I set a goal to get my temple recommend and wanted to go to the Lord's house and receive my endowment. In December of 1999 I had my interviews with my bishop and stake president and received my temple recommend. I regard the priesthood I hold and my temple recommend as two of my most valued possessions.

I also value the knowledge I have been given by my Father in Heaven. Knowledge of the gospel, the knowledge and testimony I have that all of this is real. My testimony is strong; to me it's like having a true knowledge. I have witnessed miracles in my life. I have seen this gospel change people. I have seen and witnessed things that leave me no room to doubt or question any of this. I have felt the spirit of the Holy Ghost so strong in my life that it's amazing.

When I was introduced to the church's family services twelve-step substance abuse program, I dove in headfirst. I feel that perhaps the Lord saved me so that maybe I could help save someone else. If I could help even one person out of the darkness I walked through for so many years, then what I went through was somehow worth it. I do know that God inspired the twelve-step program, and this program is His. It was put here to help people cope with the problems they have.

The program can help anyone with any problem. It doesn't have to just be drugs or alcohol. I have seen it work for people that have addictions to food, pornography, sexual addictions. It really doesn't matter what it is. One thing I have come to know is that with the Lord's help, you can overcome and conquer any problem or any addiction. There is not anything or anyone the Lord can't fix. If He could heal me He can heal anyone. The only thing you need is a sincere desire to change. If you have admitted to yourself that you have a problem that needs fixing, and the desire to change is there, then you're on the right path.

If you have made it through this story and got to this point, there has to be something that prompted you to read this. Either you or someone close to you is suffering as I once did. The main reason I wrote this story was to let others know that there is a better way to live your life. If someone would have told me ten years ago that I would straighten out my life the way I have, and be going to church and going to the temple and holding the priesthood, I would have laughed and told them they were crazy. I am fortunately living proof that it can be done. There were several times throughout my life that I really had no hope. I figured the only way out was to continue doing what I was doing and eventually it would all end in its own time and in its own way.

Over the years I have seen many people die from drug and alcohol related instances. Recently, I went to a funeral for a good friend of mine that died from a heroin overdose. I grew up with this man and we hung out together when we were younger. Now he's gone. I couldn't help thinking when I was looking at him lying in that coffin, how easily that could have been me. He left a beautiful wife and three kids behind. I know that before my time is up in this life, I will see many more people go in similar ways.

There is an ongoing battle out there that in many ways is more brutal than any war being fought between countries, the battle of good and evil. Satan and his dark warriors are doing everything in their power to destroy as many lives as they possibly can before this world comes to a close. Don't allow them the opportunity to get you or any of your loved ones.

If there were any advise I could offer to anyone, it would be to keep your families together. Children need a mother and a father that stay together. Teach your children to be kind to each other, to be good examples to others around them. Dedicate at least one night a week for a family night. Teach them in the ways of our Lord Jesus Christ. Pray together as a family. Bring them up with knowledge of the gospel. Teach them to be obedient to the laws and to always strive to keep the commandments. Go to church with your family. If you can do these things, chances are good that your children will avoid the damaging paths that I walked for so many years.

I know that I have said it before, but the changes that have taken place in my life have restored my relationship with my kids. We are all very close and I cherish the relationship I have with all of them. I have two beautiful granddaughters that I also love very much. Because of the atonement, the miracle of forgiveness can take place in anyone's life. I am so thankful for the knowledge I have been given of all of these things.

I do want to close by bearing witness one more time that God lives. He hears us and loves us all. If you feel your life is hopeless, I beg you to get on your knees and ask Him for help. He will hear you, and you will be amazed how good things can be. God be with you.

About the Author

Randy Riggs grew up in Bountiful, Utah, a quiet small town on the outskirts of Salt Lake City. At the age of 12 his parents were divorced. This threw his normal life into a tailspin. Searching for ways to escape he started hanging out with the wrong crowd at school and turned to drugs and alcohol. This turned into a 25-year journey that no matter which way he turned brought nothing but a lot of misery and trouble.

It started out being what he thought was innocent and fun: smoking a little pot, drinking beer with friends on the weekends. It progressed into much more. After suffering severe consequences, lots of problems with the law, he finally surrendered to a higher power and found his way out. At the publishing of this story the author has been completely clean and sober going into his eighth year.

"I always thought that a life without drugs or drinking couldn't be fun. I couldn't imagine going through life without it. Being completely clean and sober has been the greatest blessing of my life".

Printed in the United States
108856LV00001B/13/A